C **T**

Recipes

compiled by
Astrid Bartlett

with nostalgic illustrations
of village life by
Trevor Mitchell

SALMON

C000103928

Index

Title page: 'Fun for Some'

Printed and published by Dorrigo, Manchester, England © Copyright

All illustrations by Trevor Mitchell ©

Somerset Casserole

Somerset is one of the best counties for producing food. It is a great area for dairy, beef and cider apples. Thanks to the lush fields, interesting herbs and meadow grasses, the beef produced here is succulent, flavoursome and hard to beat.

2 lb. braising steak cut into cubes (or a mixture of shin and chuck steak)
A knob of butter   2 onions   2 tablespoons sunflower oil   1 lb. sliced carrots
1 leek, trimmed, washed and thinly sliced   ½ swede, diced   2 crushed cloves of garlic
½ pint beef stock   1 peeled & chopped eating apple (for crunch)   ½ pint dry cider
1 peeled & chopped cooking apple (to fall)   1 small parsnip, sliced
A can of chopped tomatoes   Bay leaf   Mixed herbs or bouquet garni
Cornflower and water

Melt the butter and oil in a large, flameproof casserole. Add the chunks of cubed beef. Cook until browned. Remove from casserole. Cook the onions, leek, garlic and chopped apples gently until they soften. Add the carrots, swede and parsnip. Stir well. Return the meat to the pan along with the tomatoes, beef stock, cider, bay leaf and herbs. Stir well. Taste and adjust seasoning. Cook in a moderate over (Gas 3, 325°F/190°C) for about 2 hours. Mix a little cornflour with cold water and stir it into the dish to thicken. If you have made some dumplings (recipe page 5) add them at this stage and cook for a further 20–25 minutes with the lid firmly on the casserole. You can cook the carrots, swede and parsnips separately and use the water from them with the stock, before adding them to the casserole.

PLUM TREE FARM

NATIONAL TRUST WOODLAND WALK

DEB 69

Trevor Mitchell

Herby Dumplings

There is nothing quite like a warming stew or casserole to warm the cockles of your heart in the depths of winter. To increase the delight, why not add some tasty, filling dumplings to the dish? Not only are they delicious but will make the whole meal go further too.

4 oz. self-raising flour
2 oz. suet (either original or vegetarian)
A little salt
Some ground black pepper
About ½ - 1 teaspoon of dried mixed herbs
About 5 tablespoons of water

Place all the dry ingredients into a bowl and mix well with your fingers. Add the water.

Flour your hands and then shape into approximately 8 dumpling balls. Add the dumplings to your stew or casserole about 20 minutes before the end of cooking. Make sure you have a well-fitting lid on top.

Shepherd's Pie

On a damp and miserable autumn evening, when all you can see ahead is long, cold winter evenings, what could be more comforting, warming and tasty, than a steaming hot shepherd's pie?

About 1 lb. good lean minced lamb (you can use leftover minced, cooked lamb)
A little butter   Couple of carrots, grated or diced small   Large chopped onion
Leek, chopped small   Crushed clove garlic   Seasoning   Ground coriander
Cornflour and a little water   ½ pint beef stock (or ¼ pint stock & ¼ pint red wine)
Dried or fresh mixed herbs: a hint of rosemary and mint are both good
***Optional:* 1 tablespoon Worcestershire sauce and/or a dessertspoon of mint sauce**
***For the Topping:* Potatoes   Butter   Milk   Pepper**

Brown the minced lamb in a non-stick frying pan. Allow the fat to run out and drain well on kitchen paper. Discard the fat – not down the sink. Save it for the birds. Melt the butter and add the onion, leek, garlic and carrots. Cook gently until they begin to soften. Add the lamb to the mixture. Add the stock, Worcestershire sauce/mint sauce, ground coriander and herbs of your choice. Simmer for about half an hour. Mix the cornflour with the water and add to the mixture. Stir well until the mixture has thickened. Spoon out into an ovenproof dish. Cook the potatoes. Drain and mash with milk, butter and a little pepper. Place on top of the meat mixture. Make a pretty pattern on top by ploughing through the potato with a fork. Cook for about 20 minutes in an oven at Gas mark 6, 400°F/200°C.

Six

Cauliflower Cheese

I sympathised with early-day vegetarians as their only option to a carnivore diet always seemed to be cauliflower cheese and very little else. This recipe has a few more ingredients to pep it up a bit and make it lot tastier and interesting.

A cauliflower washed and broken into florets   2 oz. butter
A medium-sized onion, peeled and chopped
A clove of garlic, peeled and crushed   2 oz. plain flour   Approx ½ pint milk
3 oz. grated cheese   Salt and freshly ground black pepper
***For the topping:* 2 oz. grated cheese   1 oz. breadcrumbs   Snipped chives**
A little ground coriander or cayenne

Wash the cauliflower and break into separate florets. Steam – or boil – until very lightly cooked. Reserve the water. In another saucepan, melt the butter and add chopped onion and crushed garlic. Cook gently until soft. Add the flour. Stir well. Add the milk, a little at a time, stirring all the while to avoid lumps. Stir until smooth. Add some cauliflower water, just enough for flavour but not too much or the sauce will become too thin. Cook until the sauce thickens. Add the grated cheese. Taste and adjust seasoning. Place the cauliflower into a buttered ovenproof dish. Pour over the sauce. Mix the grated cheese, chives, breadcrumbs and ground coriander together and scatter over the top of the completed dish. Cook in the oven at Gas mark 5, 375°F/190°C for 10–15 minutes or until the cheese goes all gooey and the breadcrumbs, golden.

Steamed Ginger Pudding

On a freezing cold winter's day, what could be more comforting than a ginger pudding steaming away, waiting to be eaten and accompanied by a sticky toffee sauce, syrup or custard?

½ lb. plain flour	1 beaten egg
1 tsp. ground ginger	1 tbsp. syrup
1 tsp. bicarbonate of soda	4 oz. suet
3 oz. sugar	Milk

Measure the flour into bowl and add all the dry ingredients: ginger, sugar, bicarbonate of soda and suet. Stir in the beaten egg and syrup. Add sufficient milk to make a soft consistency which will drop easily from a spoon. Spoon the lot into a well-buttered 2-pint basin. Cover with greaseproof paper and steam for a couple of hours. Serve with hot custard, syrup or toffee sauce.

Toffee sauce: **4 oz. butter   6 oz. muscovado sugar   6 tbsp. double cream**

Stir the butter and sugar gently in a saucepan together until the sugar has dissolved and the butter melted. Remove from the heat. Stir in the cream and warm right through.

Trevor Mitchell

Bœuf Bourguignon

There is nothing more comforting on a chilly day than a really satisfying casserole packed with flavour. This recipe is hard to beat for its simplicity, a touch of elegance, a hint of French wine, followed by a great result and a taste that will linger on the palate and also in the mind.

2 lb. braising steak cut into bite-sized cubes (stewing steak or shin are good)
8 oz. smoked streaky bacon, snipped into strips
½ pint red wine (for an authentic dish, use Burgundy)
2 tablespoons sunflower oil   A dozen shallots   A clove of garlic, crushed
¼ pint beef stock   8 oz. button mushrooms   Bouquet garni
A dessertspoon of cornflour to thicken   A little cold water   Seasoning

Heat the oil in a sturdy saucepan or flameproof casserole. Add the meat cubes and cook until browned all over. Remove meat with a slotted spoon. Add the bacon, shallots and crushed garlic to the pan. Allow the shallots to soften slightly then remove with slotted spoon. Add the wine and the beef stock to the pan. Return all the rest of the contents – except the shallots – to the pan. Add the bouquet garni. Stir well and adjust the seasoning. Put lid on casserole and cook for about 1½ hours at Gas 3, 325°F/170°C. Remove from oven. Add the cornflour mixed with a little water and stir in. Return shallots to the casserole along with the mushrooms. Cook until beef is tender – approximately an hour.

Chicken and Tarragon Fricassée

If you have any leftover cooked chicken, here is a really tasty way of using it up.
Pull all the meat off the carcass and chop into manageable pieces. Keep the carcass
aside for making a tasty soup.

2 oz. butter   1 chopped onion   Leftover chicken pieces   Any leftover chicken gravy
4 oz. mushrooms   A few freshly chopped or dried tarragon leaves
Salt and pepper
***White sauce:* (made with the 2 oz. butter, 2 oz. plain flour and approx ½ pint milk)**

Melt the butter and cook the onion gently until it softens. Add the flour, stirring well before adding the milk, a little at a time. Blend with a balloon whisk to avoid lumps. Stir until thickened. If you have any leftover chicken gravy, add that too for extra flavour. Roughly chop the chicken into bite-sized chunks. Add the mushrooms, tarragon and chicken chunks. Taste and adjust the flavour with salt and freshly ground black pepper. Heat through. Serve with a fresh salad and tarragon-rice, made by adding a few tarragon leaves to the rice cooking water.

N.B. If you use leftover gravy it will colour the sauce to a pale brown – but it should have a lot more flavour that the usual white fricassée.

revor Mitchell

Cheese Toasties – Oven-Cooked

This is great for a quick snack: filling, satisfying and tasty.
You can alter the toppings to suit the mood.

Slices of bread for toast – brown or white and as thick or thin as you like
Cheese of your choice – basic Cheddar is always good
Tomato slices   A few twists of black pepper   Dried oregano or basil

Place the slices of bread on a baking sheet. Top with grated Cheddar cheese or slivers of an alternative hard cheese. Otherwise use chunks of diced feta or slices of a soft, sheep cheese such as Little Ryding or Shepherd's Crook. Place slices of tomato on top. Sprinkle with herbs of your choice and a little black pepper. Add a little more cheese before putting into a hot oven for about 5–10 minutes until the bread is toasted and the cheese has melted into the tomato.

Alternative topping suggestions:
Cheese and pickle   Cheese and chunks of ham   Cheese, ham and pineapple
Cheese and apple with black pepper and tarragon or mixed herbs
Cheese, tomato and chopped chives
Cheese, crushed garlic and tomato, torn fresh basil leaves and olives
Cheese, tomato and sweet peppers with mixed herbs
Cheese, olives and mixed dried herbs with a little cayenne pepper

Play around with your own ideas.

Cottage Pie

The combination of meat, potato and gravy seems to hit the comfort spot every time and is hard to beat.

2 tablespoons vegetable oil
1 large, finely chopped onion
½ pint beef stock
1 teaspoon mixed, dried herbs
Salt

1½ lb. minced beef
1 large carrot, grated or finely chopped
2 skinned and chopped tomatoes
2 tablespoons Worcestershire sauce
Pepper

A flat dessertspoon of cornflour mixed with a little cold water
Topping: 1½ lb. mashing potatoes, peeled and chunked   A sliced tomato   Butter
Milk   Grated Cheddar cheese   Parsley or basil to garnish   A little pepper

Heat the oil in a pan. Add the onion, carrot and minced beef. Cook for about five minutes until the meat is nicely browned. Drain any fat away before adding the stock, tomatoes, Worcestershire sauce, herbs and seasoning. Bring to the boil. Simmer for about three-quarters of an hour. Thicken the sauce by stirring in the cornflour and water. Spoon everything into a large buttered ovenproof dish. Allow to cool while you prepare the topping. Cook the potatoes. Mash them, adding butter, milk and pepper. Spread over the top and score with a fork. Place the sliced tomatoes over the top of the potato and sprinkle with cheese. Garnish with parsley or basil and bake for about 30–35 minutes until golden brown and sizzling right through.

Ham and Leek Pie

Once Christmas is over, your spirits may be low. If you have some leftover ham, this is a good recipe for feeding the inner man and cheering you up simultaneously. Ham goes perfectly with leek and makes a good, warm, satisfying meal. Top it with a pastry lid and you will soon be back on track again.

Some leftover ham   Leeks, well washed and cut small
Onion, peeled and chopped small   1 peeled and crushed garlic clove
Grated cheese   Seasoning   Shortcrust or chilled puff pastry
White sauce (2 oz. butter, 2 oz. plain flour, approx ½ pint milk)

Make the white sauce by melting the butter. Add the prepared chopped leeks, onion and garlic until they soften. Remove with a slotted spoon and thicken the sauce by adding the flour to the pan juices. Slowly add the milk, stirring all the time to avoid lumps. When smooth, creamy and thickened, add the chunks of ham. You probably won't need to add any salt, especially if the ham has been smoked but you may need some pepper. Place the whole mixture into an ovenproof dish. Top with pastry, make a slit in the top to allow steam to escape and bake until golden brown.

Macaroni Cheese

At the convent where I went to school, we always had fish or macaroni, on Fridays. The girl at the head of the table which seated seven, served. Macaroni was never popular with my peers. As a permanently hungry (or maybe, greedy?) teen, I taught myself to love it. It meant I could have second and third helpings. It has since become a family favourite.

4 oz. dried macaroni	2 oz. plain flour
2 oz. butter	About ½ - ¾ pint of milk
4-6 oz. grated cheese	Seasoning

Some breadcrumbs

Bring a pan of salted water to the boil. Add the macaroni and cook for about 15–20 minutes. Drain. Make a roux by melting the butter in a separate saucepan, adding the flour and mixing it in carefully to avoid lumps. Add the milk a little at a time, stirring continuously, until the sauce thickens. Add half the grated cheese and stir into the sauce. Taste and season with salt and pepper to please your palate. Tip the macaroni into the sauce. Spoon the whole lot into a buttered ovenproof dish. Mix the remaining grated cheese with the breadcrumbs and sprinkle over the top of the dish. Put into the oven to heat through and allow the top to become golden brown.

To vary the contents, add any of the following to the sauce:
Skinned tomatoes, bacon, cooked ham, crushed garlic, mustard, onion, grated nutmeg, olives, chives, parsley or anchovies.

Baked Gammon

The smell of baked gammon conjures up the warmth and welcome of a kitchen which is being used for its main purpose: cooking.

A 1½ - 2 lb gammon joint (smoked or green)
2 small bay leaves
8 peppercorns
2 teaspoons set honey
1 clove garlic split lengthways

Place a large piece of foil on a baking tin. Onto one of the cut ends of gammon, place a dollop of honey, 4 peppercorns, a slice of garlic and a bay leaf. Place this face down onto the foil. Now repeat on the other end of the gammon. Wrap the foil up and over, leaving plenty of air-space for the foil to act as a mini-oven. Bake for 20–30 minutes per lb. in the centre of an oven set at Gas mark 3, 170°C/325°F. Allow to cool in the foil. Reserve the juices. They can be frozen and used as a basic stock for soups.

Fisherman's Pie

This is a good, robust meal for winter when the days are short and the shadows and nights are long. The flavour can be altered by using smoked fish as well as white fish.

White fish of your choice (haddock, cod and pollack are all good)
A little smoked haddock (optional)   4 oz. sweetcorn
4 tomatoes, skinned and chopped   Potatoes (mashed)   About 4 oz. peas
Grated Cheddar cheese   A handful fresh or frozen prawns   Bay leaf
2 hard boiled eggs, quartered   4 peppercorns   Enough milk to cover the fish
2 oz. butter   Fish stock cube   2 oz. flour   A little more cold milk
Sliced tomato and chopped chives

Gently poach the fish in milk with bay leaf, peppercorns and fish stock cube. Once cooked, lift out the fish carefully. When cool enough, remove skin and bones. Discard along with the bay leaf and peppercorns. Flake the fish and place in a buttered ovenproof dish. Make the sauce by melting the butter in a saucepan. Stir in the flour. Add a little cold milk gradually, stirring to avoid lumps, then add the warm milk/stock and stir until sauce has thickened. Remove from heat. Add the peas, tomatoes, sweetcorn, prawns and eggs. Stir carefully. Tip the entire mixture onto the fish and try to get all the ingredients evenly distributed throughout the dish. Top with mashed potato and grated cheese. Garnish with slices of tomato and chopped chives. Cook in the oven until thoroughly heated through. It's ready when the cheese turns gooey, and golden.

Trevor Mitchell

Bread and Butter Pudding

Our elder grandson William, is in charge of constructing this recipe. He likes the crusts left on and prefers cinnamon to the usual dried fruit which his younger brother Ed, favours. So, he makes one long pudding - with dried fruit at one end and cinnamon-dredged bread at the other to please each of them. I cook it under his instruction.

6 slices white bread
Enough butter to cover the bread – probably about 2 oz.
3 oz. mixed dried fruit – sultanas, raisins, currants
2 oz. sugar   2 eggs   1 pint milk

Butter the bread and cut into triangles, fingers or just neat slices. Line a buttered ovenproof dish with a third of the slices. Sprinkle the dried fruit over and then put an identical layer on top. Beat the eggs with the milk and stir in the sugar. Pour about two-thirds of the egg and milk mixture over the contents of the dish. Finish with a final layer of bread and butter. Tip the rest of the milk and egg mix over. Bake in a slow oven for about an hour to allow the bread to absorb the liquid. If you like a crunchy top, pop it into a hot oven for the final few minutes. A sprinkle of lemon zest or nutmeg added just before cooking gives an interesting flavour.

Meatloaf

There are so many different versions of this simple but tasty comfort food. Some use mushrooms and tomatoes, others celery and yet others, Dijon mustard. This is a simple version – so you can get on and enjoy the fruits of your labour, all the sooner.

**1½ lb. lean, minced beef   4 or 5 rashers streaky bacon   1 onion, finely chopped
3 crushed cloves of garlic   3 oz. breadcrumbs   1 grated carrot
Worcester sauce   Beaten egg   Salt   Pepper   A tin of chopped tomatoes
A mixture of dried or freshly chopped herbs of your choice**

Except for the bacon, combine all the ingredients together in a big bowl and mix until you have an even consistency throughout. Place the mixture into a buttered loaf-tin lined with baking parchment. Place the rashers across the width and over the top of the mixture, tucking the ends down the side. Bake at Gas 5, 375°F/190°C until thoroughly cooked through – about and hour or so.

Alternatively, use cold, lean, cooked minced beef. Sauté the vegetables (except the tinned tomatoes) until soft. Allow to cool. Once cool, add all the ingredients together. Place into loaf-tin and top with streaky bacon. Bake in the oven for about 30–45 minutes until cooked through and the loaf is firm. As the beef has previously been cooked, there will be very little fat.

Rabbit Stew

You can't really beat a good rabbit stew for ticking all the comfort boxes. It makes a pleasant change from the ubiquitous chicken and always comes out tasting good.

One rabbit, jointed   Smoked streaky bacon   A knob of butter   1 clove crushed garlic
4 oz. smoked streaky bacon   8 shallots   4 oz. pitted prunes   ½ pint dry cider*
1 leek chopped small   1 bay leaf   Seasoning   Bouquet garni or mixed herbs**
A little cornflour mixed in cold water

Melt the butter in a sturdy, flameproof casserole. Brown the pieces of rabbit. Add the bacon and cook for a few minutes. Remove and place on kitchen paper to drain. Add the shallots and heat gently for about three minutes. Return the rabbit to the casserole. Add the prunes, cider, bay leaf and herbs of your choice. Season with salt and pepper.

Bring to the boil. Cover with a lid and cook for about 1½ hours at about Gas 3, 325°F/170°C until tender. If the gravy needs to be thickened, mix a little cornflour with water and stir into the dish. For an even richer stew, you could add sliced carrot, button mushrooms and tomatoes, at the point when you add the prunes, etc.

Try red or white wine instead of cider to ring the changes. Experiment.
**You can mix your own herbs using a couple of sprigs each of tarragon, thyme and parsley.*

Stuffed Baked Apple

Some of the simplest meals give the most satisfaction. For this recipe all that is needed is a good big baking apple and plenty of interesting dried fruits, perhaps a little sugar and some spice for the filling.

One large baking apple such as Bramley, cored but not peeled
A mixture of sultanas, currants and raisins   A little demerara or muscovado sugar
A little cinnamon or mixed spice   A little water   A glacé cherry

Core the apple. Place on a buttered ovenproof baking dish. Make sure the centre of the apple, where the core used to be, is big enough to accommodate lots of filling. Mix the dried fruits together. Drop them into the centre of the apple where the core had been. Sprinkle with a little sugar mixed with cinnamon or mixed spice. Pour a small amount of water onto the mixture. Top with a glacé cherry. Place in a medium hot oven (Gas 5, 375°F/190°C) and cook until the apple just begins to split and the juices become soft, like runny toffee. Serve with custard, cream, maple syrup or yoghurt.

You can ring the changes by exchanging the dried fruits for mincemeat or topping the original recipe with grated cheese – a great accompaniment to apple. The apple can be scored with four equally distanced downward strokes to avoid it from splitting. However, I like to see it split naturally.

'Parcel for Canal Cottage'

Trevor Mitchell

Venison in Red Wine with Quince Jelly

Gary is a regular stallholder at Wells market. He is delightful, cheery and has a wonderful selection of game, from pheasant to venison and lots of other wild meats in between. It's difficult to pass his stall without being tempted to buy…

Olive oil & butter   2 dessertspoons quince jelly   Venison haunch   Sprig of rosemary
2 onions   Couple of sprigs thyme   2 crushed cloves garlic   1 bay leaf   Smoked bacon
3 carrots, washed and sliced   ¼ pint beef or game stock   A dozen juniper berries
½ pint red wine   Bouquet garni   6 prunes   Sprig marjoram
6 dried apricots   A little plain flour   Pepper   Salt

Ideally, marinade the meat overnight in olive oil and red wine with herbs and garlic. Brown the meat all over in a heavy saucepan with a mixture of butter and olive oil. Remove the meat and gently cook the bacon, onions and crushed garlic until the onions soften. Remove and put aside with the meat. Thicken the juices in the pan with a tablespoon of flour. Add the stock and red wine gradually, stirring all the time. Replace the cooked ingredients. Add the carrots, prunes, apricots, berries, herbs and jelly. Stir well. Taste and adjust seasoning. Bring to the boil and place in a slow oven for three hours or so until tender. The longer and slower the cook, the more tender and flavoursome it will be.

Cheese and Onion Herb Bread or Rolls

Who doesn't love the smell of baking bread? It must equal that of bacon cooking and freshly ground coffee for bringing on that wonderful feeling of welcome, comfort … and home.

9 fl. oz. warm milk	**1 lb. strong white flour**
1½ tsp. salt	**1½ tsp. sugar**
1 oz. butter	**Pinch of cayenne pepper (chilli powder)**
½ tsp. mustard powder	**½ tsp. fast action dried yeast**
4 oz. grated Cheddar cheese	**1 onion, finely chopped**
1 tsp. mixed dried herbs	

Warm the milk while you measure and mix all the dry ingredients together in a large bowl. Make a well in the centre and draw all the ingredients towards the centre of the bowl until you have a manageable ball of dough. Turn the dough out onto a floured surface and knead until silky smooth. Allow it to rise in a warm, draught-free place until doubled in size. Knock it back and re-knead for a couple of minutes before shaping into a round (if making bread) or 12 rolls. Place on a buttered baking tray. Allow to rise for a further 15 minutes or so. Bake the loaf in a hot oven (Gas mark 8, 450°F/230°C) for about 30 minutes, then lower the heat (Gas 6, 400°F/200°C) and bake for a further 20 minutes. If it starts to brown too much, cover with foil. You will need to reduce the cooking time accordingly, if making rolls.

Twenty-Seven

Leek and Potato Soup

Soup is a wonderful winter warmer, it can lift the spirits –
just at the time of year when you may need comforting most of all.

3 leeks, washed and sliced
1 lb. potatoes, peeled and diced
2 oz. butter
Seasoning

1 chopped onion
1½ - 1¾ pints chicken stock
Chopped chives/parsley for garnish

Wash the leeks well. I usually split them lengthways to get out any grit trapped between the leaves. Snip or cut leeks into ½ inch lengths. Chop the onion. Melt the butter in a sturdy saucepan and throw in the onion and leeks. Allow to cook gently until they soften a little – approximately 15–20 minutes. Put the chicken stock into another saucepan and add the diced potatoes. Simmer until cooked. Once cooked, add the leeks and onion to the potato. Allow to cool slightly. Add the milk and sieve or put the whole lot through a blender. Reheat without boiling and garnish with chopped chives or parsley.

A bowl of grated cheese mixed with parsley or chives to sprinkle on top of the soup once it is served up, makes it extra delicious.

Butternut Squash Soup

*All hot soups have that satisfying, comfort factor – none more so than
butternut squash – with a few added extras.*

1 lb. peeled butternut squash, de-seeded and chopped
2 oz. butter   8 oz. potatoes
2 onions   2 carrots, peeled and diced
Crushed garlic   Half a dried red chilli, de-seeded
2 pints chicken stock   1 teaspoon paprika
Salt and pepper
Some chopped chives for garnish

Melt the butter in a large, sturdy saucepan. Add the onions and garlic. Cook
gently for about 5 minutes until they soften. Add the prepared squash,
potatoes, carrots and chicken stock. Add the paprika and piece of chilli. Bring
to the boil. Allow to simmer gently with the lid on for about 35 minutes.
Remove from heat and discard the chilli. Allow to cool a bit. Pour the soup
into a blender and whizz up. Taste and adjust seasoning with salt and pepper.
Before serving, reheat gently and garnish with the chopped chives. Serve with
a good crusty granary roll or chunk of bread.

Fish Soup

The "Fish Boys" at Wells market are very obliging. They always let me have any bones or fish heads to make a good, tasty stock. The soup can be as simple or complex as you like to make it. It's fun to put in as much variety as possible, such as squid tentacles.

For the fish stock:

Fish heads, bones and skin from white fish such as haddock, cod or pollack
1 onion, cut into quarters   Bay leaf   Approximately a pint of water
Couple of chopped celery sticks   A few sprigs parsley   Dried thyme
¼ pint dry white wine   Seasoning   A few prawn shells

Put all the above into a large saucepan and simmer for about 20 minutes. Strain through a sieve. Reserve the stock. Taste and season accordingly.

For the soup:

2 tablespoons olive oil   14 oz. tin of tomatoes   1 lb. of white fish skinned and flaked
½ teaspoon dried basil   2 potatoes, peeled and chopped small
1 tablespoon fresh lemon juice   3 cloves crushed garlic   Salt and freshly ground pepper
Your prepared fish stock   2 tablespoons chopped parsley
Any other interesting fishy things such as squid, prawns, scallops (or even one of those packs of chilled mixed fish bits – if you have no access to a fresh-fish fishmonger)

Put the oil into a robust saucepan and add the chopped potato and crushed garlic. Cook gently for about 5 minutes making sure the garlic doesn't burn. Add fish stock, flaked fish and tomatoes. Add the dried basil and squeeze of lemon. Simmer gently for 15 minutes. Check seasoning and garnish with chopped parsley.

Fruit Scones

Scones! What greater comfort is there than a split fruit scone, spread with creamy butter? A welcome treat any time of year. For extra indulgence, try topping it off with a little home-made raspberry or strawberry jam and a dollop of clotted cream. (Send for the cholesterol police!)

8 oz. plain flour	2 oz. British butter
2 oz. sugar	2 oz. currants
2 oz. sultanas	1 teaspoon cream of tartar
½ teaspoon bicarbonate of soda	Pinch of salt
Milk to mix	

Rub the butter into the flour until the mixture resembles fine breadcrumbs. Add the sugar, salt, bicarbonate of soda and cream of tartar. Finger until it is evenly mixed. Make a small well in the centre. Add a little milk to form a soft dough. Knead lightly and add the currants and sultanas. Roll out to about ½ inch thick. Cut into rounds with an upturned glass or a biscuit cutter. It should make about 10 scones. Place on a buttered baking tray. Bake at Gas 7 (425°F/220°C) for about 10 minutes until golden and well risen.

'Spring in their heels'

Trevor Mitchell

Coffee Cake

This is the favourite cake of one of my grandsons. It's the one with which
he chooses to celebrate his birthday. His brother prefers banana cake.
Neither likes the other's choice of cake, which is a clever way of ensuring
they each get more of their own favourite cake on their own special day.

4 oz. sieved self-raising flour   2 eggs   4 oz. British butter   1 teaspoon baking powder
4 oz. sugar   1 tablespoon instant coffee   1 tablespoon hot water

Whisk the butter and sugar together until light and creamy. Beat the eggs and
whisk them into the first mixture. Add the flour and baking powder. Beat well
into the mixture. Dissolve the coffee in the hot water. Add to the rest of the
ingredients and beat well until consistent throughout. Divide mixture between
two buttered sandwich tins lined with baking parchment. Bake in the centre of
the oven, for about 30 minutes at Gas mark 3, 325°F/170°C. Once cooked, cool
on a wire rack. Sandwich together with the filling of your choice – such as
coffee butter-icing, orange/lemon curd, raspberry jam or just plain whipped
double cream. It's up to you.

For the coffee butter-icing filling:
Fork 1-2 oz. icing sugar into 1-2 oz. softened butter until well incorporated.
Dissolve a teaspoon of instant coffee in as small amount of hot water as possible
and pour into the mixture. Mix until smooth.

Chunky Choc Squares

Chocolate seems to be the ultimate comfort food to turn to when the spirits are low. This is simple to make, very chocolatey and hits the spot pretty quickly to alleviate hunger and bring pleasure to the palate and comfort to the troubled soul.

**3 eggs   7 oz. soft, dark brown sugar   6 oz. self-raising flour
2 oz. cocoa powder (dark drinking chocolate)
5 fl. oz. sunflower oil   A couple of handfuls of cranberries
About 4-6 squares of 70% plain dark cocoa chocolate, bashed small***

Whisk the eggs and sugar together until pale and creamy. Add the oil and whisk into the mix. Sieve the flour and cocoa powder into the mixture. As it is very dusty at this stage, mix gently with a large spoon, not an electric whisk. Put the chocolate into a polythene bag and bash hard into small chunks, with a rolling pin. Add the broken chocolate and two-thirds of the cranberries to the mixture. Stir well and spoon out into a well buttered 8–9 inch baking square. Dot the top with the leftover cranberries. Cook for about 25 minutes at Gas mark 4, 350°F/180°C. Allow to cool before cutting into chunks

* *Intense orange – or mint – dark chocolate are good substitutes for the plain dark chocolate.*

COAL AND COKE *Deliveries*

S.Irving & Sons
COAL MERCHANT
HAULAGE CONTRACTOR
DOBSTONE
Phone
ROFFORD 21

Bedford

BHL 742

Trevor Mitchell

Christmas Flapjacks

I love Christmas and all the food preparation involved. It gives me the perfect excuse to hide away in the kitchen and make it look as if I'm working, when all I am really doing is indulging my enjoyment of cooking and keeping out of the cold. Once the air is scented with warm cinnamon and mixed spice, then I know for sure, Christmas cannot be far away.

1 tablespoon golden syrup	**4 oz. currants**
4 oz. demerara sugar	**1 teaspoon mixed spice or cinnamon**
6 oz. butter	**Orange zest**
8 oz. porridge oats	**12 halved glacé cherries**
4 oz. dates, chopped small	**A handful of raisins**

Over a gentle heat, melt the butter, sugar and syrup in a saucepan. Once melted, remove the saucepan from the heat. Stir in the orange zest and spice(s) of your choice. Add the chopped dates, raisins, currants and glacé cherries. Stir well. Finally, add the oats and give it all a really good stir. Tip the contents into a buttered baking tin. Cook for about 20–25 minutes in a moderately hot oven, Gas 4, 350°F/180°C, until golden brown. Cool for a while in the tin before cutting into fingers or squares. Allow to cool completely before storing in an airtight container and hiding them away until they are ready to be shared around.

Spiced Fairings

As a newly-wed, this was the very first recipe my next-door neighbour gave me. It is still in the old spiral-backed book I copied it into. The book is now covered in butter splodges, flour and syrup but has remained a firm family favourite for over 45 years.

2 tablespoons syrup	**6 oz. butter**
12 oz. self-raising flour	**6 oz. sugar**
Orange or lemon zest	**2 pinches bicarbonate of soda**
1 teaspoon each of: ground ginger, cinnamon or mixed spice	

Melt butter and syrup in a large saucepan. Add zest of your choice. Remove pan from heat. Add sugar, flour and bicarbonate soda. Stir well. If you are making all the same flavour, add 2 teaspoons of your desired spice, otherwise divide mixture into three and add a teaspoon of each spice to each dollop of mixture. Roll out thinly. Cut into shapes with a biscuit cutter or upturned glass. Place biscuits on a buttered baking sheet; cook in several batches. Leave space between each biscuit as they tend to spread. Cook for approximately 5 minutes. Watch they don't burn. Allow to cool before removing and storing in an airtight container. Hide them until ready for use.

Orange and Ginger Biscuits with Honey and Currants

Where is the first place we head to when we need a quick fix for sugary comfort? Frequently it is the biscuit tin. These simple-to-make biscuits fit the bill perfectly and are popular with all generations. Just rolling out the mixture is therapeutic and brings comfort and satisfaction.

5 oz. butter	1½ teaspoons ginger
5 oz. sugar	A handful of currants or raisins
1 tablespoon honey	Zest of orange or lemon
	8 oz. plain flour

Whisk the flour, butter and sugar in a bowl. Add the honey and whisk again. Add the zest, ginger and dried fruit. Squish together with your fingers to make a soft, pliable ball. Place onto a lightly floured worktop and knead well. Roll out. Select your biscuit cutter. Place biscuits onto a buttered baking sheet. Cook for about 5–10 minutes, until golden brown. Store in an airtight jar or tin – preferably out of sight or they'll disappear far too quickly.

Currently there are all sorts of different sized and shaped biscuit cutters: stars, hearts, rounds, squares, pigs, hens, gingerbread men and women, but you can improvise. I frequently use just an upturned glass.

Brandy Snaps

There is nothing quite like a touch of decadence to lift the spirits. What can be more decadent than a cream-filled brandy snap – or two?

4 oz. plain flour	**4 oz. golden syrup**
4 oz. butter	**Teaspoon ground ginger**
4 oz. sugar	**Juice of half a lemon**

Melt the butter in a pan with the sugar and syrup. Remove from heat. Add the flour, ginger, lemon juice and beat well. Drop teaspoons of the mixture about 2–3 inches apart onto a buttered baking sheet. Bake in the centre of a moderately hot oven until golden.

Take care not to overcook or they will burn at the edges. Allow to cool slightly before rolling each around the handle of a buttered wooden spoon. You can make them pointed at one end like a miniature ice cream cone or leave them open-ended at both ends (to allow more filling). Allow to cool completely before filling with special whipped cream.

For the special whipped cream:
Whisk a beaten egg white   In a separate bowl whip ¼ pint double cream
Grate a little zest of lemon into the cream
Sieve a little icing sugar into the cream. Stir the zest and icing sugar into the cream
Add the whisked egg white to the cream mixture and stir well.

'Early Birds'

Trevor Mitchell

Caramel Custard

Caramel and custard. What could be a better combination?
I don't know any man who doesn't adore custard.

3 oz. sugar   4 tbsp. water

Mix sugar and water in a saucepan, stir until it boils. Simmer until golden brown. Pour into a large buttered, fireproof soufflé dish or separate small ramekin dishes. Allow to cool.

For the custard:
¾ pint milk
4 eggs
1 oz. sugar

Blend the eggs with the sugar. Warm the milk and pour the mixture over the eggs and sugar. Blend well. Pour the resulting custard through a sieve onto the caramel. Place the soufflé dish or ramekins in a baking tin. Put some water into the baking tin (or use a bain marie), to reach about half-way up the side of the dish or ramekins. Bake in a slow oven (Gas 3, 325°F/170°C) for about ¾ hour to an hour or until the custard has set. Allow to cool before turning out.

Fruit Crumble

Crumbles are good any time of year, but during the autumn and winter one is most likely to appreciate their warm comfort, especially with a topping of thick, creamy custard. The filling will depend on what fruits you have available, either freshly harvested or from your deep freeze.

6 oz. self-raising flour
3 oz. sugar
3 oz. butter, roughly cut into small cubes or pieces

Some fruits such as rhubarb, may need to be cooked gently before adding the crumble. Weigh all the ingredients into a bowl. Finger the butter into the flour and sugar until it resembles fine breadcrumbs. If necessary, cook the fruit of your choice in a saucepan. Once cooked, taste and adjust with a little sugar. With a slotted spoon, transfer the fruit into a buttered ovenproof baking dish. Sprinkle the crumble over the fruit and bake until the top is a pale, golden brown. Serve with hot custard, cream or yoghurt. The crumble can be served hot or cold and is particularly good with thick, creamy, ewes' milk yoghurt. A little cinnamon added to a plain apple crumble will enhances the flavour.

Suggestions for the fruit filling:

Apple, either solo or with any of the following fruits: loganberry, blackberry, raspberry, strawberry, blackcurrant. Plum, rhubarb and pear-apple also make good fillings for crumbles.

Trevor Mitchell

Rum and Raisin Ice Cream with Coffee

As with chocolate, ice cream seems to be one of those special foods we turn to for comfort. Don't ask me why – apart from the fact it is delicious Maybe it helps to freeze our emotions and stops them in their tracks. Who knows?

3 oz. raisins   3 tablespoons rum
1 tablespoon instant coffee, dissolved in as small amount of boiling water as possible
Give the raisins a good soak in the rum, preferably overnight.
For the custard base: **½ pint milk   4 egg yolks   4 oz. sugar   ½ pint double cream**

Make the custard by pouring the milk into a saucepan. Heat gently to boiling point. Beat the sugar and egg yolks together in a bowl. While still beating, pour the hot milk over the sugar and egg yolk mixture. Return the mixture to the pan and keep stirring until the custard thickens. Don't let it boil or it will separate. Allow to cool completely and then stir in the cream. Add the raisins soaked in rum and then pour in the coffee. Whisk as much air into the mixture as possible. Put into a sterilised lidded tub or container and then into the deep freezer. When ice cream is part frozen, rewhisk as this will help it to remain a softer mix. Repeat the whisking a couple more times if possible. You can ring the changes by substituting brandy for rum and sultanas for raisins. With alcohol in the ice cream, you don't get those frozen shards.

Quince Jelly

We have two varieties of quince: one is a round-fruited Japanese quince and growing up the front of the house. The other is a 'real quince' with pear-shaped fruits and growing in the hen-run-cum-orchard. Either fruit is good for this recipe. The colour of the finished jelly is a beautiful clear, topaz orange.

2 lb. quinces, washed and chopped up but not peeled or cored
2 pints water – if the fruit is ripe – and 3 pints if under-ripe fruit is used
Sugar

If the quinces are very ripe you may need the juice of a lemon to help it set

Chop the fruit into chunks. Place them in a large saucepan. Pour over the water.

Simmer fruit until soft. Strain through a jelly bag. Measure the liquid and allow 1 lb. sugar for every pint of liquid. Stir the sugar in to the juice. Boil rapidly until set.

Savoury Autumn Medley

Autumn is a great time of year for harvesting all those wonderful end-of-season fruits and vegetables. There are still lots of interesting herbs around too and they will add that 'je ne sais quoi' to any dish.

A knob of butter **1 courgette/marrow peeled and diced**
2 onions, chopped **Garlic, crushed**
2 apples, peeled and cored **Tomatoes, skins removed**
Ground coriander **Seasoning**
A pinch of demerara sugar
Herbs of your choice:
Rosemary, marjoram, thyme, parsley, basil, tarragon, sage
If you like a bit of heat, you can add a small piece of red, de-seeded chilli

Melt the butter in a big pan and add the onions, apples and garlic. Cook until soft but not brown. Add the courgette, the herbs of your choice and the rest of the ingredients including the chilli – if you want a bit of heat. Allow to simmer gently until soft and mushy. Season and adjust the flavour. Serve as a stand-alone dish or to accompany different meats. Certain herbs go better with certain meats such as sage with pork, rosemary with lamb and basil with beef, as a rough rule of thumb. Experiment. You'll find it's fun.

METRIC CONVERSIONS

The weights, measures and oven temperatures used in the preceding recipes can be easily converted to their metric equivalents. The conversions listed below are only approximate, having been rounded up or down as may be appropriate.

Weights

Avoirdupois	Metric
1 oz.	just under 30 grams
4 oz. (¼ lb.)	app. 115 grams
8 oz. (½ lb.)	app. 230 grams
1 lb.	454 grams

Liquid Measures

Imperial	Metric
1 tablespoon (liquid only)	20 millilitres
1 fl. oz.	app. 30 millilitres
1 gill (¼ pt.)	app. 145 millilitres
½ pt.	app. 285 millilitres
1 pt.	app. 570 millilitres
1 qt.	app. 1.140 litres

Oven Temperatures

	°Fahrenheit	Gas Mark	°Celsius
Slow	300	2	150
	325	3	170
Moderate	350	4	180
	375	5	190
	400	6	200
Hot	425	7	220
	450	8	230
	475	9	240

Flour as specified in these recipes refers to plain flour unless otherwise described.